FANCY CYCLING

How to obtain a good bicycle.

WRITE THE

EADIE MFG. CO., LIMITED,

REDDITCH.

FANCY CYCLING

TRICK RIDING FOR AMATEURS

BY

ISABEL MARKS

ILLUSTRATED

1901

Published in Great Britain in 2013 by Old House books & maps
Midland House, West Way, Botley, Oxford OX2 0PH, United Kingdom.
4301 21st Street, Suite 220B, Long Island City, NY 11101, USA.
Website: www.oldhousebooks.co.uk

Facsimile of original book held in the Science Museum Library.
Produced under licence from SCMG Enterprises Ltd.
Digital files © Science Museum/Science & Society Picture Library.
Every purchase supports the museum.

The Science Museum Library is one of the world's great research centres,
consisting of over 500,000 original works on the history and social aspects of
science, technology and medicine. The collection includes works by scientists
from Leonardo Da Vinci, Newton and Einstein as well as quirky 'how to'
manuals and original patents.

A CIP catalogue record for this book is available from the British Library.

ISBN-13: 978 1 90840 271 4

Originally published in 1901 by Sands & Company, London.
Printed in China through Worldprint Ltd.

13 14 15 16 17   10 9 8 7 6 5 4 3 2 1

PREFACE

IN the following pages it will be my humble endeavour to give an account of the many graceful, daring, and altogether fascinating feats which may be accomplished by any rider possessed of an ordinary amount of nerve, the virtue of determination, and a few spare moments secure from the rude intrusion of unsympathising spectators.

It may safely be assumed that this same practice of trick riding does not diminish the zest for country excursions, nor the pleasures and pains of the annual tour, for to the ardent cyclist no side of the sport is devoid of interest, and among the most ardent the merry trickster prominently figures. More especially are such riders fitted to cope with the road difficulties presented by those mountainous regions whose charms appeal so strongly to the lover of beautiful scenery; to them ascents present no difficulties, to them descents are as naught. Very pretty is it to see two ladies, secure in the knowledge of each other's skill, confident with the trust born of tried experience of each other's capacity, coasting side by side, their hold of handle-bars relinquished, their bicycles moving as one, their figures gently swaying in graceful unison, their fingers lightly touching each other's shoulders, their eyes bright with the joy of motion and with the pleasure of congenial comradeship.

This class of rider is naturally *facile princeps* in threading the intricacies of congested traffic in crowded thoroughfares.

Eyes trained accurately to measure distances and muscles accustomed to prompt obedience are especially able to cope with the exigencies of our crowded thoroughfares. When watching the stream of cyclists amidst the sea of vehicles and horses it is easy to distinguish between the ordinary rider and the expert. These latter may be known by the accuracy of their serpentine curves amidst the openings out of, meeting, and overtaking traffic ; by their correct steering and, by the coolness with which, further progress being temporarily barred, the front wheel is right-angled, and a stationary balance maintained.

Last, but perhaps not least, to these practical advantages must be added the saving quality of grace, the acquisition of a perfect balance, of a correct position, and of exact ankle action, which should be to the cyclist even as Mecca to the follower of the Prophet—the goal of his desire.

Therefore I trust that this unworthy effort may further popularise the gentle cult, and that it may result in an extension of the already numerous ranks of its accomplished votaries.

CONTENTS

CHAPTER VI

CHAPTER VII

INTRODUCTORY CHAPTER

TRICK cycling, in addition to many other virtues, possesses the enviable, if negative, quality of requiring neither the adoption of a special garb nor of a special place for its indulgence.

Either for practice or performance a cycling school is naturally most to be commended, whether taking into consideration excellence of surface, absence of the too interested small boy, or the presence of skilled instructors whose services smooth the difficulties of the beginner's somewhat stony path. Therefore is it well to avail one's self of these advantages, if it be possible to do so. Failing this resource, a club ground, the asphalted space usually to be found at the base of flats or other large buildings, a garden, a secluded road, a public park, or any other place free from traffic will serve the purpose. Thus the scant leisure of a busy individual may be immediately utilised, and a spare hour entirely devoted to the special object in view without loss of valuable time spent in travelling.

The ordinary roadster will serve equally well for fancy riding, although the ideal machine for this purpose should perhaps be built with strengthened frame, stronger and straighter forks, a head well raked back, and a short wheel base to allow of quick turns, short circles, and an instant obedience.

The gear should be low, about 50. No inconvenience

would result from the very quick ankling thereby necessitated should speed be desired, as a fast rate of progress is quite a negligible quantity in trick cycling.

Regarding position and reach, experts as usual agree to disagree, but the preponderance of opinion certainly favours a forward position and a not too extended reach, the latter being not only physically injurious, but also tending to impart undue length and rigidity to the figure, thereby lessening the graceful unison of movement that should exist between the rider and the machine. In connection with the make of the mount, the imperative mood may only be used as regards the shape of the handle-bar, which *must* be short to allow of uninterrupted lateral leg movement. The upward curving variety, albeit an abomination on the road, is here neither unsuitable nor inelegant. Retarding influences being restricted to the downward pressure of the feet exerted upon the rising pedal, the brake, being in this instance useless (and never under any circumstances ornamental), can be discarded.

Body movement and ankling are among the primary factors that make for success. They add a threefold grace to riding, producing swing, accuracy in steering, and, mark well this attribute, regularity of movement. This regularity, which tends so greatly to lessen the labour of propulsion, is at first difficult to acquire; a tendency to unconscious back-pedalling being an all but universal result of the slipshod method of teaching so greatly in vogue, or perhaps it would be more correct to say, the want of any teaching at all. This pernicious habit is at once exposed and cured by the use of a free wheel; fitted with a *one-point* back-pedalling brake, where the slightest check imparted to the rising pedal is transmitted to the brake, with, at first, a somewhat disconcerting result. The experience in ankling thus forced upon the rider is, however, of great eventual benefit, and quite repays preliminary discomforts. The ability to turn within a narrow circle, or at an acute angle, and accurate steering represent the first milestone gained upon the road of progress. To join a class of musical rides is an agreeable method by which to acquire this knowledge. Failing this resource, I advise the following method :—Choose a level piece of ground, place a large stone or other distinguishing mark for the centre of your circle. When mounted, hold the handles lightly, sit well back in the saddle, upon which the weight of the body should rest entirely, leaving the handle-bar entirely free for steering purposes, and carry the pedals round quietly and evenly without exerting undue pressure upon them at any point of the stroke. Lean towards the inner edge of the circle, leaving the head of the machine freedom to follow the movements of body and feet, by which the steering is so much and so beneficially affected. Humour the machine. Does it show a tendency to heel over to the right, bend in that direction, for the balance will then be easily and gracefully maintained. By observing these directions difficulties will soon vanish. As proficiency is obtained, gradually lessen the size of your circles until a tendency to touch mother earth with the pedal points to the attainment of the limit of possibility in that direction. Learn to circle both to right and to left, the latter being the more difficult to acquire. Wise and careful folks practise these turns at first slowly and with discretion, then, as proficiency rewards diligence, pace is increased and the circles are described quickly, easily, and gracefully, with pleasure both to the rider and to the onlooker, for these sweeping movements have much charm. Another useful elementary exercise consists in the placing of small obstacles at arranged and equal distances one from the other, and in winding in and out amongst them. When the obstacles separated by but four or five feet can be safely negotiated, you are well on your way to obtain a thorough mastery over the restive steed. These bending evolutions particularly demonstrate the utility and convenience of a low gear and a short wheel base for this class of cycling.

The stationary balance is a feat which all and every cyclist should most certainly cultivate. An explanation of this evolution will be found on page 25. Its application is almost as useful in traffic as in trick riding. In many a tight place it has been the means of averting disaster, for it gives such complete control that even when surrounded by innumerable horses and vehicles, the sudden closing in of an open space ahead means but a cessation from labour, and a comfortable quiescence in the existing state of affairs. Its acquisition involving not the slightest chance of personal injury, the novice can overcome preliminary difficulties without extraneous aid and quite alone, an assertion which cannot be made of some of the feats about to be described, in the attainment of which a proper caution must be exercised and professional or other help invoked if needed.

The third preliminary manœuvre, which the trick rider must acquire in the early stages of his progress along the road of knowledge, is the capacity of riding without the aid of the handles. This is best learnt when going at a fair pace. Sit as usual well back on the saddle and boldly remove both hands, pedalling meanwhile evenly and continuously, retaining a steady seat and allowing the body to follow the swing of the machine. Pedal manipulation is at first extensively used to assist the steering, although when correct body movement has been attained, it is well to allow the feet to uninterruptedly and evenly assist progress and to contribute towards the steering as little as possible. At first the magnetic power of the handle-bar is difficult to resist, but when hold has been completely relinquished even for a second, another step has been taken in the right direction. For by the exercise of perseverance and pluck, aided by even pedalling, the period of relinquishment will gradually lengthen until you will be able to go rejoicing on your way as much at ease minus as plus the aid of the handles. Then will remain in fact but the second part of the evolution to accomplish, which is the ability to circle when in the former position. This is the more difficult of the two varieties to acquire, on account of the inclining of both rider and machine towards the inner side of the curve to be described, an inclination which engenders a not unnatural fear of a spill. But the equilibrium is quite easily maintained if courage be not lacking to resist that appeal to the handle-bar which circumstances seem to prescribe. Observe the same rules as when riding in circles and in figures of eight in the usual manner, and proficiency will surely follow. Having mastered this preliminary training, a secure foundation has been laid for the attainment of the novel and difficult feats which are open to the accomplished trick cyclist.

Want of space has caused the exclusion of much interesting matter, for new evolutions and combinations follow ever upon practice. In addition to this charm, this favoured pastime enables its followers to pursue the bent of their own individual inclinations, to adapt their proceedings to their own capacity, and to benefit by the originality of their own ideas. Many roads lead to Rome, and different performers frequently attain the same result by different means; therefore when any one special description of an illustration is given it must be taken to represent that individual's special procedure. My endeavour to visibly represent the accomplishment of the various tricks mentioned here would have remained in the nimbus of the unattainable save for the kindly help of those good enough to give time and trouble to the furtherance of my purpose of illustrating the letterpress by means of photographs. To them, and to those who have lent the seclusion of their clubs and of their cycling schools, who have aided and abetted me in this my desire, I beg to present my heartiest thanks, and to assure them of my appreciation of the great help they have thereby afforded me.

In the following chapters I have endeavoured to explain the illustrations as concisely and fully as possible, believing that such a course will be of much advantage to those desirous of following the example of the riders here depicted.

Man being liable to err, mere woman following meekly in his wake can hardly hope to escape the contagion of his example. Therefore I humbly crave your kind indulgence for faults both of omission and commission that may interfere with the due and proper presentment of the interesting subject upon which I have ventured to dilate, perhaps somewhat after the fashion of those who intrude where angels fear to tread. May my insignificant efforts be of some little service to the merry band of tricksters; may the track of their wheels be ever increasingly present in the land.

A Near-side Mount

Place the left foot on the left pedal. Lean upon the handle-bar, and rise into the saddle whilst passing the right foot over the frame of the machine to catch the rising right pedal.

Dismount over the Handle-Bar

When speed has been reduced, rise on the left pedal when it is at its lowest point, and bring the right leg over the handle-bar to the ground.

CHAPTER I

Our Little Ones

Coasting

Side-Riding

Riding "hands off"

WHEN riding at a fair pace remove the hands from the
handles, pedalling meanwhile very evenly and keeping the
body well back on the saddle. Steer by body movement.
The hands can either be folded behind the back or across
the chest. In sunny weather one can mount with a parasol
in the hand, and when riding comfortably "hands off" it is
possible to open the sunshade and to cycle, thus comfortably
protected from the heat. Our model also occasionally
indulges in an arm-in-arm ride with a little companion,
holding with the disengaged hand the parasol, which can
be either given to her by a kind friend at the proper
moment, or else opened in the manner described above.

Riding Side-Saddle

To effect this, stand on left side of the machine, holding the handles in the usual manner. Place the left foot on the left pedal, tilting the bicycle slightly to the right to assist in maintaining its equilibrium. Push gently with the right foot, rise quietly into the saddle on rising left pedal, keeping both body and feet on the left side, and pedal on with the left foot. This little lady has reversed the procedure, already described, this being a matter entirely at the rider's discretion, for in this as in nearly every other trick a mount can be made on either side of the machine, although the left side is more generally used for this purpose.

At Goy's School, Porchester Hall, Pickering Place, Bayswater.

Coasting on Saddle

When riding in the usual manner, relinquish the right pedal, stand upon the left and lift the right foot up to the saddle, pressing meanwhile upon the handle-bar to assist the balance. When steady, bring the left knee up to the saddle and gradually rise to standing position.

Unicorn Driving

The driver and off-side wheeler mount simultaneously, the former holding the reins in the left hand. The leader is driven into position by another rider, who, when the latter is in his place, hands the leader's reins to the driver of the team, passing them over the wheelers' shoulders into the coachman's left hand. The same kind office is performed for the near-side wheeler, who thereupon joins hands with his companion. The team must keep their relative distances, more especially when rounding corners. The length of the reins is regulated by raising or lowering the hand in which they are held.

The Old Style and the New

Driven and driver mount simultaneously, the former suiting in this case his movements to the latter's, and drive in the usual manner, the adult being careful to suit his pace to that of his juvenile companion.

Stationary Balance

Gradually reduce pace until movement is hardly percep-
tible. Then angle the front wheel in the direction of whichever pedal is foremost when this action is about to be made.
Press downwards alternately upon either pedal, this movement causing a gentle oscillation of the chain, by which
means the slight movement necessary for the equilibrium of

the machine is maintained. The inexperienced at first find some difficulty in attaining and preserving the right pedal pressure, but a little perseverance and an utter disregard of the abrupt movements of the back wheel usual in such circumstances are all that is required to ensure success. If the heel of the foot is rested upon the bracket better control of the machine is obtained. Revert to normal position by restoring the front wheel to its original straight line and pedalling on.

CHAPTER II

The Evolution of the Coast

Coasting on Handle-Bar

WHEN riding at speed slip the feet over the handle-bar, simultaneously swinging the body forward until the former can be placed upon the foot-rests and the latter upon the handle-bar. The saddle is grasped by the left hand, the right retaining hold of the handle-bar. To enable effective control of the machine to be maintained, it is necessary to manipulate both wheels. Steer by body and wheel movements.

Coasting upon Foot-Rests of Front Forks

Mount facing the steering wheel by placing the right foot upon the right pedal, which should be well forward, and push off with left from the ground, the left pedal being caught as it rises. When speed is obtained, put the right foot on the foot-rest and the right hand on the saddle, the left remaining on the handle-bar. The left foot is next placed on the other foot-rest, and the cramped position till then assumed, with knees doubled-up under the handle-bar, is abandoned for a standing posture. Steer by saddle and handle-bar.

Side Coasting upon Step and Foot-Rest

Mount in the usual manner. When speed is obtained, rise from the saddle, bring the right foot from behind the machine over to the step, remove the left foot from the pedal to the foot-rest upon the same side as the step, and relinquish hold of the handle-bar. When steady, rise to full height. Steer by pressure upon foot-rest, assisting the balance by arm movement.

Coasting—Kneeling upon Saddle

Mount in usual manner. When riding at the speed deemed necessary by the rider, release the right pedal, press upon the left, rising meanwhile from the saddle and placing upon it the right knee; steady yourself by resting weight upon handle-bar, then raise the left knee beside its fellow and coast.

Coasting—Steering with Feet on Handle-Bar

A preliminary acquaintance with foot-rest steering is necessary before attempting this extension of foot-steering. When riding in the usual manner, relinquish the pedals, place ball of feet on the handle-bar, and, removing the hands, clasp them around the knees.

At Goy's School, Porchester Hall.

Coasting Backwards—Sitting Side-Saddle on Top Stay

[SEE NEXT PAGE

Coasting Backwards—Sitting Side-Saddle on Top Stay

This feat necessarily implies a prior knowledge of riding backwards. (See page 44.) When proceeding in that manner, lift the right leg over the saddle, sit on the top stay, and, releasing the left pedal, coast. When desirous of pedalling on, actuate left pedal.

At Emerson's School, Dril Hall, Heath Street, Hampstead.

Coasting—Knees on Handle-Bar, Feet on Saddle

[SEE NEXT PAGE

Coasting—Knees on Handle-Bar, Feet on Saddle

Mount in the usual manner. When riding at speed bring the right leg over the saddle to the left side of the machine. During the next half-revolution of the left pedal place the right foot upon the saddle, then remove the left from pedal to saddle. When quite steady drop the knees upon the handle-bar and fold the arms. Steer by drawing in whichever knee is in the direction of the fall which appears to be imminent.

At Jarvis' School, 81 Euston Road.

Coasting with One Foot on Saddle

When riding at speed, release the right pedal and place the foot on the top tube. Then bring left foot up to the saddle, upon which the right foot is then placed. When steady, balance on one foot.

Coasting on Chest

Start in the usual manner. When riding shift the left foot to the step, which alteration in position brings the body behind the saddle, when the pedals being released, the above attitude can be assumed. Steering is effected by means of the handle-bar.

Coasting—Standing on Saddle "hands off"

When the left pedal is almost at the highest point, step on to the saddle with the right foot and immediately place the left upon the left handle, from which the left hand is removed. Acquire a comfortable position upon the saddle, and, steadying yourself, remove the right hand from the handle-bar and rise to full height. This difficult feat requires great skill and nimble movements, as in the earlier stages of the proceedings hasty and unexpected dismounts may frequently occur.

CHAPTER III

The Ramifications of the Stationary Balance

At Queen's Club.

Forward-side Stationary Balance

Forward-side Stationary Balance

PLACE the left pedal at its lowest point, right angle the front wheel, leaning the machine over to the right; place the right hand upon the centre of the handle-bar, the left on the tyre of the front wheel, the right foot upon the left pedal, and balance, using left foot as an aid to equilibrium.

Backward Stationary Balance

Stand facing the saddle with back to the handle-bar, holding the handles with both hands; mount by the left pedal, slightly resting the body against the handle-bar and pedal on. When steady, angle the front wheel, and manipulate the pedals in the usual way. Steer by means of the handle-bar.

At Emerson's School, Drill Hall, Heath Street, Hampstead.

(a) Backward Stationary Balance

(*a*) and (*b*).   Mount in the usual manner.   When a perfect balance has been obtained, take the match from the

At Emerson's School, Drill Hall, Heath Street, Hampstead.

(b) Lighting Lamp

pocket, gently remove the lamp from the bracket, open
same, strike the match thereon and light; when the wick
is well burning, replace the lamp on bracket. All movements must be made very gently.

(c) Knitting on Wheel

(*c*) and (*d*). Mount holding the ball of wool in one hand, and balance. When steady, place the ball on the saddle, and knit. When work is finished, stick the needles through

(d) Backward Stationary Balance

the ball, place latter on the saddle, and ride off.   Those who wish to follow this lady's example must first attain great proficiency of balance.

At Emerson's School, Heath Street, Hampstead.

(e) Backward Stationary Balance—"Removing Jacket"

(*e*) Mount as usual. On obtaining perfect stationary balance, gently remove the jacket. This manœuvre requires careful watching of the back wheel, for unless caution is observed the necessary movements will disturb the balance.

The graceful rider here depicted holds the record for stationary balance, which she has uninterruptedly maintained for two hours.

There are many other pretty tricks in which the stationary balance can be utilised. A game of ball can be played by two friends who have brought their machines to a standstill opposite to each other. The ball, which is carried either in one hand or in the pocket, can be thrown, caught, and returned many times. The young lady who has kindly given us so many examples of her skill awheel has enjoyed many times this new version of Nausicaa's pet game. Nor has she neglected the claims of the shuttle-cock, although the movements of the feathered playthings are in such circumstances apt to be erratic, and therefore difficult to foretell. A cup of tea taken when resting awheel after these amusements proves doubly refreshing, and pussy has been known to make the saddle her resting-place when her mistress has been enjoying her afternoon meal in this manner.

At Porchester Hall, Pickering Place, Westbourne Grove.

Stationary Balance—inside Frame

When stationary, bring the right foot quickly over the frame, resting it against the lower tube. Slip from the saddle, at the same time taking hold of the front wheel with the left hand, and of the top stay with the right. Balance is effected by exerting pressure on the left pedal and by slightly oscillating the steering wheel in whichever direction a fall threatens. Before resuming normal position depress left pedal.

Balancing on Bottom Bracket

Place the ball of right foot on bottom bracket and the heel on left chain stay, incline the machine slightly to the right and remove the left foot from the ground. Either use the left leg as a balance-rod by extending or withdrawing that limb as occasion demands, or place the point of the left foot between two of the spokes of the front wheel, and by gentle oscillation of the latter help to preserve stationary position.

Stationary Balance—Sitting on Handle-Bar

Attain the stationary position whilst seated upon the saddle with feet on pedals. Then move forward and sit upon the handle-bar; take first one foot from one pedal and place it on a spoke of the front wheel, then perform the same operation with the other. Equilibrium is maintained by alternately lightly depressing either foot, which action imparts a slight movement to the front wheel.

Stationary Balance—"Hands off" and Feet on Tyre of Front Wheel

When pace has been sufficiently slowed, the front wheel is right-angled in the ordinary manner. Upon the tyre are placed the feet. By gentle movements they cause their support to almost imperceptibly oscillate, thus replacing the usual chain movement and transferring activity from the back to the front wheel, an effect produced in a somewhat similar manner in the trick last described. When the machine is perfectly balanced, remove and fold hands.

Stationary Balance on Front Wheel Facing Handle-Bar

Stand, facing the handle - bar, over the front wheel. Mount by the left pedal when well forward, catching the right as it rises, and steering by means of the handle-bar. When desirous of reducing speed, either lean weight on the tyre or back pedal; the stationary balance is produced by manipulating cranks in the usual way and angling front wheel.

Stationary Balance—Foot on Saddle and Pedal

This evolution is effected by a threefold simultaneous movement. When riding in the ordinary manner choose the moment, when the left pedal is at its lowest point, to rise from the saddle to press upon the pedal and to angle the front wheel. At the same second of time lean forward and catch hold of the front wheel and place the right foot upon the saddle, the most important point being the ability to grasp the wheel, which ability guarantees the equilibrium and balance of machine and rider. The wheel is, of course, moved in whichever direction a fall threatens.

CHAPTER IV

Heads and Posts, Tilting at the Ring (Sword), Tent-Pegging

Assault	*Tilting at the Ring*
Cavalry Cut	*Tent-Pegging*
Cut at Infantry	

THE sword and lance used for heads and posts, tilting at the ring, and tent-pegging are in Neville's School, whose skilful pupils are here depicted, similar to those used at the Agricultural Hall by competing teams at the Military Tournaments, and the procedure adopted is that laid down for Cavalry Drill, 1898.

At Neville's School, Drill Hall, Davies Street, Berkeley Square.

Heads and Posts

Proceedings commence by the " engage." This is effected by carrying the sword smartly to the right with the arm bent and the elbow behind the hand, with the point of the sword advanced and in front of the left eye, the "fort" —that half of the blade near the hilt—covering the centre of the body, both head and body being turned towards the right front. The "assault" is then delivered by a strong, back cut, with arm as high as the neck. The back of the sword is placed upon the right shoulder, with the hand to the right and as high as the cheek, the elbow being under the hand, and the head and body turned towards the right front.

The remaining parts of the exercise consist of cuts and points delivered on either side. The sword is held with the middle knuckles in the direction of the edge in all cuts and guards, the grip of the handle being maintained by the thumb and fingers around it.

Heads and Posts

The first cut is to the right at cavalry, this most estimable arm of the service being represented by the head and post.

Tilting at the Ring

The second is a point to the left at the ring which is attached by a string to its supporting post, and which must be taken upon the point of the sword and dropped over the left shoulder.

The third cut is to the right at cavalry.

At Neville's School, Drill Hall, Davies Street, Berkeley Square.

Heads and Posts

The fourth is yet another cut but at the sister arm, the infantry being represented by a post three feet high.

The fifth is a point at infantry, namely, a ball lying upon the ground.

Points are given for time and style as well as the successful execution of the various feats. The necks should be cut neatly through so that the heads fall smartly to the ground. The length of the course depends naturally upon circumstance, but, if practicable, it should be 100 yards in a straight course.

Heads and Posts

Tent-Pegging

The peg should be 12 inches long and 3 inches wide and about 1 inch thick, 6 inches being left above ground; on a wooden floor the peg should be only 6 inches long and placed on a "rest." When mounted, the lance is carried at the "engage"—that is to say, it is grasped at the "balance" and held under the hollow of the right arm with the thumb to the right and the knuckles underneath. Upon arriving within 15 yards from the peg the lance should be lowered to the right side, the position of the hand being altered, the thumb being uppermost and the back of the hand to the right, and the point is directed into the peg with the

Tent-Pegging

body lowered as much as possible. No jabbing nor stabbing with an erect body is permissible, the impetus given to the bent body by the speed of the bicycle should be sufficient to drive the point home. To avoid shock to the wrist when the peg is taken the butt of the lance should be recovered over the left shoulder. This is effected by leaving the point in the peg and trailing the weapon behind with a perfectly loose arm, the butt resting against the left shoulder. After a "take" the lance is brought to a "carry," with the peg still adhering to the point and carried to the end of the "run" to count as a "take."

CHAPTER V

Deeds of Derring-do

Butterfly Dance

THIS pretty idea originated with Mr. Neville, who has patented the special necessary form of garment, which is of chiffon decorated with clusters of spangles, and cut in a peculiar fashion. Inserted within the folds are supports of wood with grips for the hands in order to effect the required manipulation needed to illustrate a butterfly's

Butterfly Dance

flight. When off the machine the dress is like an ordinary short, plain gown, falling in pretty folds from the shoulder. When first worn at one of the Abingdon Drill Hall gymkhanas a head ornament fitted with an electric light was used, the effect being very lovely when combined with the graceful movements of the rider, her white draperies and the coloured lights thrown upon the floating apparition. Mount in usual manner, and when steady, release hold of

Butterfly Dance

the handles. Raise the arms, when the hands, which are
placed in the supports, can at will cause the superfluous
width of the robe to assume most lovely and graceful
shapes. In fact, a skirt dance awheel is simulated.

At Neville's School, Drill Hall, Davies Street, Berkeley Square.

Picking up Handkerchief

Mount in usual manner, holding the handkerchief in the hand. Throw it out straight in front when the right pedal is descending. At the following revolution let the body descend with the descending right pedal, and when the latter is at its lowest point pick up the objective.

Riding One Machine, Leading Two

Ride in usual manner towards the bicycles, one of which is laid on the left, the other on the right, side, the handle-bars being inclined towards the rider. Stoop with descending left pedal, and when it is at the lowest point take hold of the prone machine by the left handle, swing it up and then remove hold to centre of bar. After another revolution of the pedal come to a halt, balancing yourself on both machines, whose front tyres touch. Stoop down with descending right pedal and raise the second machine in the same manner as the first. Having manœuvred the machines into the positions depicted in illustration on following page, resume pedalling—a not very easy matter be it said, as the front wheel of the ridden machine is apt to swing to either side and to collide with its neighbours; the position of the

Riding One Machine, Leading Two

pedal is also unfavourable to movement, a fact which
does not lessen difficulties. When riding, the led machines
are kept slightly in the rear, always at the same respective
distances from their industrious comrade; and in describ-
ing figures of eight and small circles the outer machine
must be allowed to forge a little ahead and the inner be
held back a trifle to the rear. This feat is very difficult
to accomplish, and should be attempted with caution.

At Neville's School, Drill Hall, Davies Street, Berkeley Square.

Riding minus Handle-Bar

Mount with the assistance of the lamp bracket. When quite steady, remove the hands and steer practically by body movement only, the feet helping but little in that respect. Even when taking sharp turns and short circles the wheels are in almost perfect alignment, the rider producing the necessary movement by leaning *very* pronouncedly towards the inner side of the circle to be described. This is not an evolution to be attempted without due consideration of the difficulties to be overcome, for to execute eights and to take sharp turns when riding "hands off" is comparatively easy, but to deprive one's self of the possibility of resorting when in difficulties to the assistance of the handle-bar as a means of restoring equilibrium is quite a different matter—a matter which should be well considered before reflection is converted into fact. Much skill is required to ride a machine minus handle-bar, even when the balance is assisted by holding the head with one hand, and without that aid to the skill required for such a feat must be added the qualities of judgment and of courage. The lamp bracket must be left in its usual position, although, of course, the lamp is conspicuous by its absence. A handkerchief or some protecting cover must be wrapped round the right hand, for in order to mount unassisted the head must be grasped, and the edges of the socket are sharp, and therefore are liable to produce painful abrasions of the skin. When seated, the dress can, if necessary, be arranged without causing inconvenience. When going at speed the hand should be removed from the head, and the steering should be effected by body movement, the feet assisting little, if at all, in that respect.

A Risky Stationary Balance

Of all the stationary balances herein described, this is the one that exacts the greatest amount of nerve from the performer. The distance of the pedals from the floor is a little over five feet, and consequently the trickster must look down from a height of at least ten feet. This intervening space between one's self and the floor is quite sufficient to produce giddiness or a feeling of discomfort when one is standing erect upon the somewhat insecure support of two small pedals; therefore this feat should be attempted only by those who rejoice in the possession of a head not likely to be affected by such a consideration. Nor should this particular trick be either practised or performed without the presence of a teacher or a friend who is experienced enough to be able to diagnose the symptoms pointing to a fall, and so prevent any damage otherwise likely to be the result of such an occurrence. Any ordinary table will serve as a rest for the machine, provided it is long enough to afford the necessary support, and stands steadily and equitably upon its four legs. The chairs should be placed upon the table at a distance from each other representing the wheel base of the particular machine to be used in the performance of this trick. Heavy weights are put within the framework of the chairs to lessen the risk of their slipping upon the surface of the table. The machine is then lifted and placed upon the chairs, after which the rider gets upon the table by means of another chair, and is assisted to mount. Should the machine not be in a convenient position it is lifted up with the performer seated in the saddle and shifted until the desired end is attained.

This effected, the rider manipulates the pedals in the usual manner until a satisfactory balance has been attained, when the tyre of the steering wheel, after it has been angled, will be found to be touching at one point the back

A Risky Stationary Balance

of the chair upon which it stands. The crucial point is then reached when the hold of the handle-bar is relinquished, and equilibrium must be maintained without its support. This being safely accomplished, the sunshade, which has been until then held in the hand, is opened and raised above the head. A much easier method of executing this trick is to place two chairs at the requisite interval. The machine is mounted whilst standing in the ordinary manner upon the ground. The rider mounts in the usual way, and is lifted (machine included) upon the two chairs placed to receive their burden. Then comfortably elevated, the stationary balance can be easily assumed.

Skating Awheel, Riding in Usual Manner

Ride side by side. When ready, release the handles and
clasp hands, allowing sufficient space between the machines
for handle - bars and pedals to escape touching. When
taking curves, the outer rider increases, the inner decreases,
speed. Steering is effected by body movement aided by
pedal manipulation.

Skating Backwards Seated on Handle-Bar

Mount facing the saddle by either left or right pedal. When a fair speed has been obtained, raise yourself to sitting posture upon the handle-bar. When quite steady, release the handle-bars and take the hands of your partner, who has hitherto been riding alongside.

It may be of interest to readers to mention that the clever executants of the last ten tricks are all pupils of Mr. Neville.

At Neville's School, Drill Hall, Davies Street, Berkeley Square.

Riding Backwards Seated on Handle-Bar

Mount in usual manner for ordinary backward riding. Let the body rise with rising pedal and sit upon the handle-bar. When quite steady, fold the arms.

f

At Queen's Club, West Kensington.

Pedalling on Reversed Machine

This particular trick can be performed equally well either in school or out in the open. In the latter case it is well to select, if possible, a lawn or any other piece of grass as a resting-place for the machine, for otherwise the plating may suffer. If attempted out of doors, care should be taken, if the wind be blowing, to select a sheltered spot, where its disturbing influence would be least felt, as the elevated position of the performer affords ample opportunity of his being affected by this inconvenience. This particular instance of the cyclist's skill is not often attempted, for to stand upon the revolving pedals when the machine is placed in the position depicted in the illustration is about as excellent an example of practice aided by natural capacity in this direction, overcoming all obstacles, as it is possible to secure.

To attain the desired result the bicycle is placed resting upon the handles and the saddle. The rider stands facing the back wheel. In order to mount he must bring the left foot over the bracket and place it upon the right pedal, holding meanwhile the back wheel to prevent any movement of the bicycle whilst he is so occupied, and thus mount by the right pedal, the right foot being then brought up to the disengaged pedal. The hold of the wheel is then relaxed, and the pedals are made to revolve, carrying, of course, round with them the feet of the doughty performer, whose sole support they constitute. The pedalling must be very regularly performed, and the balance can be assisted, if necessary, by arm movement.

At Queen's Club, West Kensington.

Taking a Rest

This little picture explains itself.

Riding Backwards Seated on Side-Saddle

Of riding backwards there are two varieties. The first and more general consists, as we have already seen, of using the handle-bar as a support for the body, the saddle being in this instance quite neglected for that purpose. An erect position, with the back to the handle-bar, being adopted, the term riding backwards is used to designate this particular manner of cycling, although this description of the attitude in question is distinctly an incorrect one. It is true that the face is turned towards the contrary direction to that in which the machine is proceeding, but the latter is really running in the ordinary way, and the pedals are being manipulated in the usual manner. To cycle, when seated on the saddle, in the opposite direction to that which is faced is a very different matter, for in that case not only is the actuation of the pedals very different but the steering is most puzzling to the beginner. The latter, however, unlike the pedalling, is in reality quite simple, the front wheel being used for that purpose in the same manner as when riding forwards. This fact is at first difficult to be grasped, as the tendency is towards a contrary action, and when once this stumbling-block in the path of progress has been removed much progress has been made. But the difficulties of the pedalling are only to be overcome by constant practice and the exercise of much perseverance, the acquisition of a good method of clawing up the pedal being particularly trying to the patience. The mount also calls for much skill; and this combination of difficulties is the reason why this excellent feat so seldom forms part of the amateur's *rôle*. Some beginners favour the practice of mounting by pushing off with the hand when awheel from some stationary object, such as a wall or, better still, a post. Others assume the stationary balance and then attempt to ride backwards from that position. Either method may be tried according as fancy dictates. When the art of riding backwards has been learned the following method of mounting should be acquired:—The experimentor should stand behind the machine and place the left foot upon the left pedal, which should be rather more than half-way up, and should push off with the right, and rising into the saddle start immediately upon his retrograde way. An adept can adopt almost any position when riding backwards. Our very clever friend favours a side-saddle posture, availing himself, as is usual in side-riding, of the services of one foot only, the other being placed upon the foot-rest. By the adoption of this method the steering and the balance are naturally rendered more difficult.

At Porchester Hall.

Riding on One Wheel

Riding on One Wheel

The performance of this trick does not involve the acquisition of so much skill as the last of which mention was made. The mount is effected in the usual way. When the rider wishes to make an alteration in the manner of his going, and to attain the desired position of cycling upon one wheel only, he presses hard upon whichever pedal happens to be foremost at the moment when action is taken upon this decision, pulling at the same time upon the handle-bar. A tendency to fall forward is sometimes developed by these movements, and sometimes the reverse feeling is experienced. Either of these undesirable results can be prevented by the adoption of suitable precautions. For the forward tendency, which is caused by an undue elevation of the front wheel, a matter frequently occurring to the beginner, and which results in an involuntary dismount, forced upon the rider by the necessity he experiences of stepping off backwards, the remedy is easy and efficacious. It consists of back pedalling, which simple act will at once correct the error of judgment which has been caused by inexperience. When the tendency is to fall forward the reverse action is taken, and pedalling on is the order of the day. The steering is the same as that used when riding without touching the handle-bars. As to position, we are told that the body should be well held back upon the saddle, and the arms kept almost straight. The effect upon the beholder of seeing several men riding in this manner one behind the other is very startling, and the introduction of such an item in a gymkhana programme would be productive of much mirth, besides possessing the merit of originality.

Riding with Right Leg through Frame

When riding backwards swing the right leg over saddle to the left side of the machine, place the right foot on the right pedal, both legs being on the left side, and ride on.

Riding outside Frame

Mount by right pedal with back to the handle-bar when the crank is well forward, and catch the left pedal as it rises, holding the handle-bar well in the centre. The mount must be effected very smartly, as the whole weight of the body rests upon the hands until the feet touch the pedal, consequently balance is difficult to maintain. Steer by handle-bar and pedals. It is advisable to be careful when negotiating corners or taking sharp curves.

Riding Standing upon Pedals

Mount in usual manner. When going at speed, rise from the saddle, release the handles, leaning the body well forward over the handle-bar. Steer by body movement, aided occasionally in this task by the feet.

Riding inside Frame

When riding at a fair speed, slip from the saddle and sit on the tubes of the frame.

Riding on Mud-Guard

Stand behind the back wheel. Place the right foot on the right pedal when it is nearly at the highest point, push off with the left, and pedal on.

At Sheen House Club, East Sheen.

Riding Seated on Saddle, Back to Handle-Bar

Mount, standing with the back to the handles, by left pedal, rising into the saddle with the rising pedal. Steer in the usual way, and when riding at speed, release the hold of the handle-bar and fold the arms.

At Sheen House Club, East Sheen.

Mounting with Front Raised Wheel

Hold the machine vertically in above position. Place one foot on the pedal and spring into the saddle, pulling on the handle-bar to prevent the steering wheel falling too abruptly, for should it strike the ground too hard the forks would suffer.

At Sheen House Club, East Sheen.

Changing Machines

When performing combined tricks it is needless to say that it is a great advantage to the performers to be thoroughly conversant with each other's idiosyncracies, and to possess unlimited confidence in each other's capacity. The trick about to be described is perhaps quite unique, for although ladies have been known to exchange without dismounting their own machine upon which they had, up

to the moment of their decision, been riding in favour of
one they had been leading, yet that is a very different
matter from executing the double trick about to be
described. The executants, whose counterfeit presentiments
are before you, are very expert at this and many other
combined tricks. They have no fixed formula to meet the
exigencies of the case in question, but vary the proceedings
from time to time. Upon the occasion when the accompany-
ing photograph was taken they adopted the following evolutions to accomplish their purpose. The rider upon the left-
hand machine we will call A ; he upon the right shall be B.
A commences proceedings by lifting the left foot from the
pedal to the chain-stay, and continues the movement by
then swinging it over the back of the saddle to the project-
ing part of the hub. B now begins to act. He rises from
the saddle, letting the handle-bar swing round and pass
between his knees, and shifting his right foot to the chain-
wheel. To A the next manœuvre is entrusted. He puts
his right leg over B's machine, and his right foot on the
right pedal, removing at the same time the left foot from
the pedal to the chain-wheel of his own machine, or to any
other convenient support thereon that may happen to be
handy. B thereupon straightens the handle-bar, removing
his left leg over the top tube to the left side of A's bicycle,
and places his left foot upon the left pedal, and the right
foot upon the right pedal. A bringing the right foot over
to B's machine the exchange of machines is completed, and
each rides off with his new possession.

At Sheen House Club, East Sheen.

Vaulting over Handle-Bar

Rise on the pedals when they are horizontal, place the hands in centre of the handle-bar, and spring from the pedals over the front wheel to the ground. Turn quickly, and catch the machine as it falls.

A Venturesome Trio

The riders cycle holding each other's handles. The passenger mounts from the back of moving machines, wearing very light shoes out of consideration for his supporters. He climbs on to their shoulders, and steadying himself, rises to full length.

CHAPTER VI

Combined Pastimes

Skipping

THE "rope" is a piece of cane, which can be bought for sixpence. It is usually decorated at either end by a bow of ribbon. Mount, holding in one hand the cane. When riding at fair speed, release the handles, take an end of the rope in either hand and gently lower the cane a little in advance of the front wheel, under which it is then passed on its way to be treated in a similar manner by the back wheel. Having thus been carried along the ground the length of the bicycle, it is raised over the head to resume the previous movements. Steering is by body and feet movements.

At Neville's School, Drill Hall, Davies Street, Berkeley Square.

Hoop-Skipping

Mount, holding the hoop in one hand. When riding at speed, release the handles. Raise the hoop above the head, and bring it down to the ground a trifle in advance of front wheel, which then passes over the obstacle. This effected, a nimble turn of the wrist slants the hoop towards the back wheel, beneath which it slips. It is then raised above the head to recommence the series of operations.

Riding through Hoop

Mount as described in preceding page. The mud-guard is usually removed from machine. When sufficient speed has been obtained, lean slightly forward in the saddle and slip the hoop under the front wheel, raising it beneath the lower tube of the frame to allow of the head being passed through the upper part of the hoop. The latter is then brought over the shoulder, and the hoop lowered to allow the back wheel to run over the wooden circle, which is

At Neville's School, Drill Hall, Davies Street, Berkeley Square.

Riding through Hoop

then swung to the right side of the machine and brought
forward to the front wheel to permit of the series of
operations being repeated.

Horizontal Bar Exercise

In a cycle display our old friend the clown often plays a prominent part, and it was in order to amuse an audience that the gymnast here depicted assumed his peculiar attire, which, however, does not seem to have interfered with his

Horizontal Bar Exercise

agility. Before appearing in public, the riders who undertake the onerous duties of props must thoroughly accustom themselves to the duties required of them, and to the difference in steering which the swaying weight they carry must necessarily cause. Great care is required in turning corners, and a fairly slow rate of movement will be found most suitable. On account of the face having to be extensively "made up," and for other reasons the clown's costume may not always find favour, in which case any ordinary attire will serve.

Proceedings commence by the two riders mounting simultaneously. They have but one hand free to assist in this operation, as the other is occupied in holding an end of the pole which finds a resting-place upon their shoulders,

Horizontal Bar Exercise

or, to be more exact, upon the top of the backbone at the back of the neck. The pole must be of sufficient length to allow of uninterrupted free movement on the part of the gymnast who must not, under any circumstances, come in contact with the cyclists. When the latter are quite prepared for his advent he approaches the carried bar which he lightly grasps, swinging himself into position, and is at

once ready to begin his exercise.   All his movements are of
a regular and careful nature, which consideration does not
affect the peculiar attitudes that can be assumed.

Horizontal Bar Exercise

CHAPTER VII

Side-Riding   Double Riding

Side-Riding and Coasting   *Double Riding*

Double Side-Riding

Side-Riding and Coasting.

SIDE-RIDING consists of a series of evolutions (six in number) which are executed upon the left side of the machine. They may be performed uninterruptedly, or they may be separated one from the other by a few rounds of ordinary side-saddle riding should the former course be found too fatiguing to pursue. The first of these series ends in a coast; the second in riding upon the step and the pedal; the third in riding upon the pedal only; the fourth in a coast with the left hand upon the hip; the fifth is executing eight when side-riding seated upon the saddle; and the sixth concludes with riding upon the step and the pedal with one hand resting upon the saddle.

Mount side-saddle, placing the right foot upon the left foot-rest. When going at speed cross the left foot over its fellow and (1) coast. When desirous of resuming work catch the left pedal with the left foot, rise from the saddle, and placing the right foot upon the step—(2) step and pedal—ride on. The next proceeding consists of removing the right foot from the step and letting it hang idly next the foot which is upon the pedal, (3) pedal only. This is the only evolution of the series in which there should be movement of the body, the latter stiffly rising and falling with unbent knee with the ascending and descending pedal, the steering being, as usual, effected by the handle-bar. To assist the rising pedal lean upon the handles, which should bear the weight of the body as much as possible. When tired of this method of progression replace the right foot upon the step, put the left upon the rest, and resting the left hand upon the hip, (4) coast. Resume side-riding seated upon the saddle (5) and execute figures of eights. After which, bring the right foot once more back to the step, and rising, stand upon the pedal (6) with the hand upon the saddle. For this kind of riding the machine must be fitted with step and foot-rest.

At Emerson's School, Drill Hall, Heath Street, Hampstead.

Double Side-Riding

Double Side-Riding

There are many very pretty and effective tricks capable of execution by two friends making use of one machine only, upon which to display their efficiency in the fine art of fancy cycling. Unfortunately, a great number of such feats are not particularly suitable for ladies to attempt, but as in the natural course of events trick riding continues to evolve the inventive minds among its votaries will doubtless discover many numerous and skilful combinations. Side-riding would seem to be especially adapted to attempts of this kind, as provided the riders be of about the same weight the question of balance would not seem to be affected. A machine to be suitable for the above purpose would require a step fitted to either side, and if doubts be entertained in regard to the rigidity of a lady's mount, under such circumstances a diamond-framed machine could be used. In the double side-riding, illustrated on opposite page, the ladies mount together in the following manner. The left-hand rider places her right foot upon the left pedal when it is well forward, her companion mounting by the steps both standing at the back of the machine. The latter catches the right pedal as it rises, keeping meanwhile the unoccupied foot upon the step; the former likewise utilises the step upon her side of the bicycle as a resting-place for her left foot. Weight is only allowed to be put upon the descending pedal and upon the handle-bar; the rising pedal should, in its ascending movement, lift the foot and body with it. Steering is effected by means of the handle-bar, and by body movement.

Double Riding—On Pedals and Steps

Another kind of double riding is that in which the riders confront each other, and the patient bicycle has to adapt itself to a different distribution of its load. The participants in this particular trick are representative of both sexes, and those fair cyclists who like to take their pleasure quietly will appreciate this circumstance at its proper value. This evolution is performed by Mr. Emerson in two ways. . In the one instance he and his pupil mount at the same time, she from the back of the machine, by means of the steps with which it is fitted. He stands outside the frame facing the saddle, and attains the pedals from that position. The other method of arriving at the same result is of a more elaborate nature. A pre-arranged meeting-place is decided upon, where the lady takes her stand and patiently awaits the arrival of her participant in the proceedings. He mounts alone in the manner just described, and cycles slowly to the rendezvous. When he reaches the appointed spot his partner runs alongside for a couple of seconds, then, catching hold of the saddle, she gently raises herself upon the steps, and takes her stand behind the seat. She is thus carried along resting all but imperceptibly against the saddle, her hands clasped behind her back. She must confide implicitly in the skill of the rider, and give herself up entirely to his guidance, a matter some would find more difficult than performing alone the most nerve-distressing evolutions. Eights can be executed when riding in this manner, and the stationary balance attained and discarded. The latter is, however, very difficult to do, on account of the load at the back of the machine.

SINGER CYCLES

(LADIES)

Singer Patent Free Wheels.
Singer Patent Locking Bolt.
Singer Patent Brakes, Etc

THE NEW CENTURY SENSATION.

Perfect
Combustion.
No Smell.
Easy to Ride.
Safe.
Reliable.
Simple.

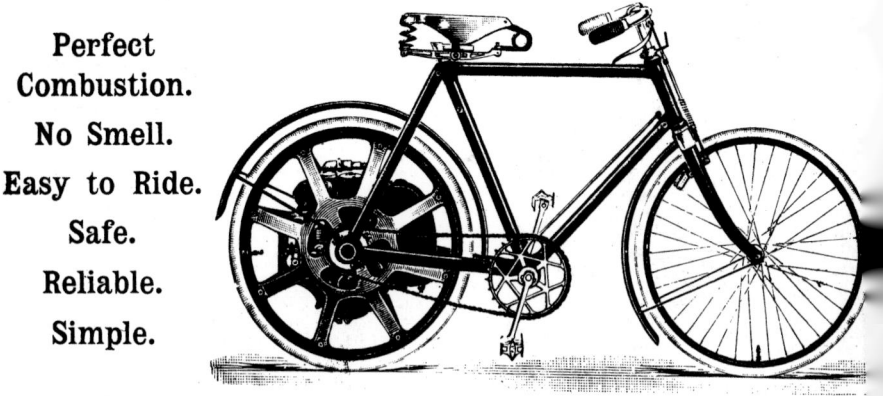

Full particulars and Lists of Gent.'s and Ladies' Motor Bicycle
and Tricycles, free on application.

Sole Makers: SINGER CYCLE CO., LTD.
LONDON: 17 HOLBORN VIADUCT.